Instructions for u

GW00455241

LET AUGMENTED REALITY CHANGE H

With your smartphone, iPad or tablet you can
use the **Neighbur Vue** app to invoke the augmented
reality experience to literally read outside the book.

neighbur

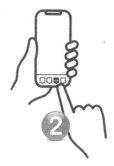

1. Notice the spelling: download the **Neighbur Vue app** from
   the **Apple App Store** or **Google Play**

2. Open and select the (vue) option

3. Point your lens at the full image with the and enjoy
   the augmented reality experience.

Go ahead and try it right now with this image from the cover
of this book.

Praise for *Return on Influence*

"This is a book that should be on every leader's shelf, whether it's wooden or digital. Susan Luke Evans delivers insights and wisdom on every page, ensuring that leaders can create a massive "return on influence". Using stories, examples and humour, her message is one that every leader needs to hear, and every team member needs to know. If you buy only one book this year, make it this one."

Alan Stevens, FPSA, PSAE, MCIPR
Past President, Global Speakers Federation
Co-Author: The Exceptional Speaker
London, UK

"In this smart and sincere guide, Susan shows how workplace culture can be positively shaped through the sharing of personal stories. Susan demonstrates her own matchless brand of story-telling in this unique perspective on leadership communications. Keep your ears open at the water-cooler!"

Hazel Smith
Freelance writer, Toronto Canada
France Today Magazine

"Susan Luke Evans has worked with leaders around the world to craft and tell stories that engage, inspire and empower their teams to deliver extraordinary outcomes. In this new how-to book Susan uses her 5-level 'Pyramid of Influence styles' to clearly demonstrate the bottom-line value of great stories."

Donald Cooper, MBA
International Speaker & Business Coach
Toronto, Canada

"When Susan Luke Evans has written a book on "influence" we should all read it! Susan has a powerful ability to influence others and I know I will be a better leader now that I have read her book."

Darci Lang
Canadian Speaker Hall of Fame Author & Speaker
Focus on the 90% – Kind Leadership

"Susan Luke Evans' wonderful book *Return on Influence* inspired me to think about where, when and how a well-told personal story might help inspire my audience, win the hearts of my prospective clients, and solve the inevitable differences with people I care about."

Shelle Rose Charvet
Author of *Forbes* Best Management Book
Words That Change Minds

"Susan has a unique ability to open your mind to greater possibilities by exploring your own, personal value. In this book she takes you on a thought-provoking and profound adventure through the causes and effects of the impact you leave on others when they experience the real you; your "Return on Influence". Susan reveals the true qualities of leadership beyond the skills and techniques taught by so many leadership books and courses. This is a must-read for anyone who wants to bridge the gap between being a leader and being a visionary."

Jayne Lowell
Co-founder, Deep Thought Strategy

"This book reveals a powerful concept called the "Return on Influence" which brings clarity to your far-reaching impact as a leader. Susan's concepts help you understand the implications of your leadership and communication style, empower you to further strengthen your position as a leader and visionary, and secure your legacy. Susan brings her global experience and wisdom, combined with her masterful story-telling acumen to create a learning experience that is as captivating as it is transformative."

Steve Lowell, CSP
2021-2022 President, Global Speakers Federation
Co-founder and Author of Deep Thought Strategy

"Susan is a coach, leader and powerhouse speaker. Her international travels resonate with my own journey as a writer, and connecting with Susan, makes me feel like the world is indeed a smaller place. Her book, ROI, *Return on Influence* is a new testament of how we should see currency as a spiritual exchange. A great book for young entrepreneurs like myself. Susan's book packs nuggets of wisdom that are unforgettable. I couldn't put this book down!"

Pashmina P.
International Best-Selling Author of
The Cappuccino Chronicles Trilogy
M.Ed International teaching, Framingham State University, Massachusetts

"Susan's influence in the world is evident in the way she connects with a number of people. She has the power to influence others and catapult them into a different perspective. A must read for every business owner."

Judy O'Beirn
Best-Selling Author of the Unwavering Strength Series
President and Founder, Hasmark Publishing International.

"Susan's book is a must-read for anyone in a leadership role: even if you already see yourself as a strong influencer, you'll benefit from her vast insight and experience. Her practical framework is a revelation which will make a profound difference to you, your team and your business."

Annabelle Beckwith
International business consultant
Best-Selling Author of Get Your Peas in A Row – 5 key factors to propel your business forward

"Susan's experience in the field of leadership over many years is what continues to keep her ahead of the game. As a European, the figures for our economy as well as the wellbeing of our staff indicate that a scary number of our employees are disengaged. This book could not have come at a better time, offering leaders a different way to change. The statistics and the disengagement results can improve through sharing real stories and personal experience. I highly recommend this approach from a masterful storyteller and leader."

Heather Waring
Founder of One Million Women Walking
Author of How Walking Saved My Life
London, UK

Return On INFLUENCE

THE NEW CURRENCY FOR LEADERS

SUSAN LUKE EVANS

Hasmark PUBLISHING INTERNATIONAL

Published by
Hasmark Publishing
www.hasmarkpublishing.com

Disclaimer
This book is designed to provide information and motivation to our readers. It is sold with the understanding that the publisher is not engaged to render any type of psychological, legal, or any other kind of professional advice. The content of each article is the sole expression and opinion of its author, and not necessarily that of the publisher. No warranties or guarantees are expressed or implied by the publisher's choice to include any of the content in this volume. Neither the publisher nor the individual author(s) shall be liable for any physical, psychological, emotional, financial, or commercial damages, including, but not limited to, special, incidental, consequential or other damages. Our views and rights are the same: You are responsible for your own choices, actions, and results.

Permission should be addressed in writing to Susan Luke Evans at susan@susanlukeevans@com

Editor: Gary Hoffman
gary@hasmarkpublishing.com

Cover Artist: Pibworth Professional Solutions
lauren@pibworthps.com

Layout Design: Anne Karklins, Kelly Kinsman
anne@hasmarkpublishing.com

ISBN 13: 978-1-989756-70-6
ISBN 10: 1989756700

FOR WARREN

*whose influence lives on through his legacy in the lives
of family, friends, and the global speaking industry*

CONTENTS

ACKNOWLEDGMENTS

How does one thank people who have been part of this book writing journey? You see, it all started over ten years ago, for a completely different reason and with a completely different focus. As is often the case, life happened, and the unfinished manuscript got put on the shelf.

I believe that things happen for a reason, even when I do not always understand the reason. Over the past ten plus years I married the love of my life, worked and traveled with him, provided care and support during his cancer journey, and kissed him goodbye as he transitioned from this life to the next on August 22, 2014. Almost immediately I went back on the road, working with hotels on 6 continents and in over fifty countries. In 2018, I finally grieved, had my own health issues, and gradually began to go back to work. And then along came COVID-19. Living alone and isolated for four plus months, I took another look at the manuscript. I realized that it needed a different focus and the result of multiple revisions, rewrites, and additions are embodied in this book.

Ten plus years means a lot of people influenced this book, both intentionally and unintentionally, directly and indirectly. Do not panic, I'm not even going to try and name them all. Yet, I would be remiss not to mention several who have been there for me during the good times and the challenging times. Without them, I might not be here.

There are many in the professional speaking communities around the world, in addition to Warren, who have been there for and with me (in no particular order): Naomi and Jim Rhode; Barbara Glanz; Pam and Jack Burks; Toni Newman and Gerry Benard; Kit Grant (who also worked with me for three years across the planet); Elizabeth George; Steve and Jayne Lowell; Donald Cooper; Alan Stevens and Heather Waring; Lindsay and Debby Adams; Cate Collins; Orlando Bowen; Joe Sherren and Kristin Arnold; Debbie Peterson; Shelle Rose Charvet; Randy Park; Rose Adams; Juri and Ulana Chabursky; Shirley Taylor; Robyn Pearce; Nabil Doss; Paul ter Wal; Dr. John Molidor; Marilynn Semonick; Shelby Yeaman; Drake Beil; Leigh Mamuad; Sam Horn; Eamonn O'Brien; Paul du Toit; Stef du Plessis; Ross Saunders; Sigi and Claudia Heider; Lou and Jonellen Heckler; Mike and Veronica Schoettler; Darci Lang; Jeff and Lydia Mowatt; Sean Weafer; Shari Bricks; Michael Kerr; Alvin and Darlene Law; Lesley Everett; Mel Sherwood; Madeleine Black; Graham Davies; Bob Gray; Stephen de Wit; Sunjay Nath and Enette Pauze; Randall Craig; Tom Stoyan and Peri Shawn; Codi Shewan; Carol Schulte; Faythe Buchanan; Ross MacKay; June Cline; Jean Houston Shore; W Mitchell; Richard Mulvey and Charlotte Kemp and so many more.

Family and friends have also been there for me, including: my mom, who left us at age 101 in 2011, she was my friend, my mentor, my role model – always willing to listen, to inspire and give me critical feedback; my awesome big brother, Tom Kilpatrick; my amazing son, Chuck Chaney and his equally amazing wife, Amy Chaney, and their children Charlotte and Luke; George Evans and Hazel Smith and their son Noah; Victoria Evans; Pete Luke; Cheryl Weaver; Richard and Mary Reinthaler;

Andrea Pollard; Sean, Joh, Jacob, and Jessica Pollard; Barbara Main; Ed and Sharon Jackson; Corinne Kelt and Alasdair Farquharson; Rosalie Fernandez; John and Yvonne Kerns; Brent and Linda Moss; Paul and Debbie Fletcher; George and Marion Mackay; Brent Knapp; Colleen Trager; Sue Longson; Kerry and David Towle and so many others scattered around the world who have influenced my life.

Of course, I would be remiss if I did not mention those friends and colleagues who have actually helped birth this book either directly or indirectly:

Judy O'Beirn and the entire team at Hasmark Publishing. They encouraged and cajoled me, gave me more homework than I ever dreamed, joined me in laughing, and I am grateful to everyone, Judy, Pashmina, Jenna, Danielle, Jenna, Amanda, Jenn and Dave.

To Lauren Pibworth and her amazing team at Pibworth Professional Solutions who designed the book cover, have been with me through multiple website iterations, and always provide HUGS on request!!

And last but certainly not least, to Jennifer Darling and her team who helped me enhance my LinkedIn profile and banner to increase my presence and coordinate it all with the website and the book.

All I did was jot down a few thoughts, stories from and lessons learned during my time as a CEO and as a consultant and coach to leaders at all levels – everyone else combined to do the "heavy lifting" and to bring this project to market. Thank You is such a simple phrase, but it is the very BEST way to express my gratitude to one and all for all things large and small that combined to result in something important to consider.

Susan Luke Evans
CSP and Global Speaking Fellow
Etobicoke, ON Canada

FOREWORD

Susan Luke Evans has been a CEO of a technology firm, coach to leaders for over thirty years, and a Certified Strategic Planner. She is known for enabling leaders to inspire their teams to high levels of performance that last.

How does she do this? She teaches them about the five levels of influence – and helps them know the difference between temporary and sustainable influence. If a leader has to prod their team to go to the next step, even if the team is "motivated," the responsibility still sits squarely on the shoulders of the leader, who can end up becoming a micro-manager and eventually burning out.

Susan elegantly lays out the 5 levels of influence: Compliance, Participation, Buy-in, Leadership and Visionary, and shows you how to find out at what level you are operating, as a leader/influencer. When you are working with your team above the "Mission – Critical line," then you have people who are fully engaged in creating success. But how can you get there?

When a leader shares WHO they are and WHY they are engaged, through sharing their story, it opens the space for everyone to participate. Susan decodes HOW to do this and demonstrates WHY it is ever more important.

After I read my dear friend Susan's book, I realized that I had not told a long-time client the full story of why I continued to work with them all these years; why it mattered to me. When I told them the story, instead of letting me go because of COVID-19, they re-engaged with me and have kept me as a consultant/trainer.

Imagine your impact when you can find the stories in you that truly convey who you are and why your mission and goals matter.

    Shelle Rose Charvet
    Author of Forbes Best Management Book
    Words That Change Minds

IN THE BEGINNING

"Every moment is a fresh beginning."
– T.S. Eliot

"It was 3 o'clock in the morning," he said as he slowly leaned forward in his chair. As he began his tale, the room was quiet. All eyes focused on this tall, handsome young man, new to the supervisory ranks of the chemical plant located in the sultry low country on the southeastern coast of the USA.

"I was out at the back of the plant, hazmat suit and all, testing the level of the water quality in the pond. I was alone, and it was very dark. As I stepped to the edge of the pond, I stretched my arm out over the edge to complete the test… when two glowing, reptile eyes popped up!"

To be continued…

The goals of successful communication are to <u>influence</u> and <u>persuade</u> as the actual communicator, and to listen actively as the receiver. Communication happens in a variety of methodologies: orally, visually, and kinesthetically. They all have common attributes in terms of how communication is given and received. And there has been a great deal written, spoken, explained, researched, and repeated, to help us understand why communication is so important to our relationships, organizations, communities, and cultures.

The case above was about *Little Timmy*, the infamous alligator that lived in the middle of the chemical plant's pond. Our soft-spoken young man continued, "I suddenly realized that it was just me, my flashlight, the testing material, and *Little Timmy*... alone, together, in the dark. Oh yeah, I realized that *Little Timmy* wasn't a big 'gator. Yet, realistically, I was well aware that even little 'gators have very big and very sharp teeth. Those eyes were sizing me up as his midnight snack. This was definitely not in my best interests."

It was summertime and humid-hot in the interior, windowless room where the group was assembled. You could have heard a pin drop as the story continued. Every person in the room already knew about *Little Timmy*. Many of them could have told a similar story. They all knew that *Little Timmy* had been living in that pond for some time, and it was not safe for anyone to be out there alone. Especially in the middle of the night. Yet, the pond had remained home to *Little Timmy* the alligator. Nothing had been done to remove *Timmy*, even after numerous notes in the daily log, and frequent conversations with management. Nothing had been done to change the procedure in order to ensure the safety of the person responsible for testing the water at that specific time – the graveyard shift. The reason was probably based on the fact that there was not a staff member designated as *Manager of Alligator Removal*.

The story of *Little Timmy* had emerged as part of a management development program, illustrating a specific concept, chosen by the storyteller. In this instance, our tall, lanky storyteller wanted to illustrate that "the plant" should make changes in unsafe procedures before someone got hurt; "they" should be more proactive in preventing accidents and paying attention to details, rather than waiting for an accident to happen.

Mission accomplished.

Great story? Maybe. True Story? Absolutely!! How did that story influence the people in the training room that day? What was the return on its influence and how did it manifest itself?

We have not seen a lot about what the return on influence is, as communicators and leaders. What follows is not "rocket science." It may be a bit of a different perspective that can help us look at the how and why of what we are doing, and how we can focus that understanding to maximize our return on influence.

THE FIVE LEVELS OF INFLUENCE THROUGH COMMUNICATION

"Never underestimate the influence you have on others."
– Laurie Buchanan

The return on a leader's influence is based on five levels. Based on my observations and experiences as a CEO, as well as working with leaders at every level, across industry lines, for 30 + years, on six continents, and in over 50 countries, here is what I've learned:

A leader begins influencing others at the level I call COMPLIANCE: this is when employees change how they behave and what they do because you told them to do it.

You know you are influencing at the COMPLIANCE level when:

- People are doing what they should do.
- For the most part they are doing things correctly.
- They are punctual. They come to work on time, take breaks on time, for the required amount of time, and they leave on time.
- They do the bare minimum to get the job done.
- The leader is operating in a more supervisory role rather than a leadership role.
- When we look deeper, we may see that there is little or no evidence of independent thinking or problem solving, and no creative thinking.

Those at this level are complying as a BEHAVIORAL response.

The second level is what I call the PARTICIPATION level: this is when changes are made selectively and temporarily, based on the way employees feel about their work, which may change from day to day.

At this level, the leader observes that:

- People appear to be more content with their work.
- They are happier and more approachable.
- They care about the outcome of the project or job, but only from the perspective of protecting their place in the company or as part of the team.

- There may be glimpses of initiative and creative input.
- Employees bring you more problems and few, if any, options or solutions.
- Their enthusiasm for the project or the job is somewhat short-lived.
- When "stuff happens" they are easily frustrated, often dropping back to the COMPLIANCE level or sometimes below that into a DYSFUNCTIONAL level.
- They are less punctual: perhaps coming in late, leaving early, taking longer breaks and maybe more sick days.
- They are obviously less productive. This happens because of the temporary nature of how they approach the project or job. When things do not happen in the way they should, or in the way they expect them to, they lose their enthusiasm.
- This is all about the NOW or how they feel. Then they function or participate in the moment.

The term "participation" used in this context refers to the increased individual participation by those at this level; albeit possibly short-lived, there is some initiative taken by these employees.

Those at this level of influence are participating because of how they feel EMOTIONALLY.

The third level is what I call the BUY-IN level. This is when employees contribute to the company because they have changed their mindset about the work they do.

You can recognize those at this level because:

- People's feelings of well-being for and about the project or the overall business are longer-term and more sustainable.
- People come to you (the leader) with more options and solutions than problems.
- They buy-in concerning the overall vision and mission of the company.
- They understand that this is all about getting the job done well and properly.
- They are more consistent and conscientious.
- You can rely on such people, and they never let you down.
- Often these are longer-term employees who have been in their positions for years. They like what they do, and they do it well.
- They do not appear to have any interest in moving up the corporate ladder or expanding their role in any way.
- They are confident in their ability to do the job and do it well.

Typically, they are at this level of influence for one of two reasons:

1) They genuinely like what they do, they are good at it, and they do not want to change; or

2) they do not believe they are able to do more, or are not confident in their ability to move forward:
    - These folks are often seen as the "diamonds in the rough" of the organization.
    - They have both the skill and the ability to move forward and become leaders in the future.
    - They need confidence, mentoring, etc.

When we ignore our "diamonds in the rough" we are not influencing others for the future of the organization. They need to be influenced to believe in their ability to do more and move to the next level.

Those at this level of influence are buying-in because they BELIEVE in themselves and their ability to do the job, as well as in the organization.

The fourth level is what I call the LEADERSHIP level. This is when employees change their mindsets based on how they feel about themselves.

You can recognize when you are influencing at the LEADERSHIP level because you, the leader, "feel" it. What that means is:

- These folks may have become your protegees.
- They often may see themselves in your position in the future.
- They have original and creative ideas.
- They can expand on your ideas.
- They may be able to finish your sentences. (That's only creepy when it's "Alexa" completing your sentences.)
- They are truly following in your footsteps (while NOT being underfoot).
- You may sometimes find yourself going to them for counsel or guidance.

Those at this level of influence are beginning to act like and be IDENTIFIED within the organization as leaders.

The highest level of influence is what I call the VISIONARY level. This is when the leader is influencing people to influence others. At this level we realize that:

- These people are seen and accepted by others in the organization as leaders.
- Other employees turn to them for guidance.
- They actively work on/try to build things that will outlive their tenure with the organization.
- Their focus is on a better, overall future for the organization.
- They may initiate programs: community, environmental, etc., not because it's part of their job, but because they're involved in building their individual LEGACY as well as that of the organization.
- They are building something much bigger than themselves.

Those who are at this level of influence are recognized as LEGACY builders, both in building their individual legacies as well as contributing to the LEGACY of the organization.

Influence Pyramid

> On the Influence Pyramid the division between the **BUY-IN level** and what I call the **LEADERSHIP and VISIONARY levels** is the **Mission Critical Line**, which may often be unrecognized by leaders.

Why do I believe it is a Mission Critical Line??

- It defines the difference between the TEMPORARY levels of influence and the SUSTAINABLE influence levels.
- Unless a leader is willing to share his/her own identity with others, his/her influence will always fall short of its potential.

Many leaders are either unaware of, or have not given much thought to, the Mission Critical Line – They:

- Influence to change behavior.
- Inspire to change how others feel.
- Convince others to "buy-in" to the mission and vision.

None of these things are BAD. However, they are all TEMPORARY, and not sustainable over the long haul. The first 3 levels are all temporary in the overall big picture of the Influence Pyramid. They are considered temporary because the outcomes may not transfer from one project or day to another.

Influencing at the top 2 levels, LEADERSHIP and VISIONARY, requires each leader to share some of his/her own PERSONAL EXPERIENCE.

In my experience, the best and most powerful way to accomplish that is through living and sharing our own stories, our experiences, or possibly the experiences of others or historical references.

Included would be 3 basic types of stories/experiences that are often found in business organizations:

- The most obvious type would be our own Personal Stories. Anecdotes or short vignettes about things that have happened to us – explain WHO we are, how we acted or reacted in a specific situation, etc.
- The second type might be called Parables, and can be described as a story that explains WHAT we do by revealing a moral (WHAT we learned/can learn), and it may often be about someone else – a relative, a co-worker, a former boss or colleague – someone with whom we have a personal connection, either directly or indirectly.
- The third type are often described as Legends or Legendary. These are the stories within the business that help explain the history or the WHY/HOW of a specific policy, procedure, marketing campaign, etc. that are found in every business, large and small.

As leaders, we can share these stories to reveal something about ourselves, our history, what we learned, why we do things the way we do; the stories reveal not only something of ourselves but more about the organization. These are the "backstories" behind the bullet points that may be seen in an onboarding presentation or manual.

Any story or experience that may help folks to "get it" more quickly is usable, as long as the "teller" relates to the story in some way – personal, parable/lesson learned, or legendary – and the story relates directly to the issue under discussion. This is not about using someone else's story as if it were your own.

This is not about using storytelling to achieve a specific desired outcome.

It is about leveraging the power of stories to elevate one's message for greater influence.

What does that mean, exactly?

The goal of a leader, at any level, is to influence others to become better: to communicate more effectively, to listen actively and with empathy, and to operate more strategically. When we influence at an inappropriate level, we are not communicating. We are either talking down to someone in a condescending manner or working above their level of understanding at that point in time.

The difficulty becomes understanding how to communicate most effectively, knowing what we know about the levels of influence, when communicating to a group of people at different levels, which describes teams, organizations, communities, and cultures.

Most leaders understand how to influence others to:

- Do this because I told you to do it.
- Do this because you will have a more pleasant time at work.
- Do this because you "get" that it is good for the organization (and by extension, good for YOU).

These are the basic reasons we communicate and influence others. We truly do not expect much in return. When given a variety of specific cultures or environments, we may be able to influence others to change their behavior, learn new skill sets, and/or make more informed decisions in an efficient and logical manner.

These are all good outcomes. Generally speaking, however, they produce short-term results, which often fade over time. There is nothing wrong with these short-term results and they are a necessary part of supervisory management.

The actual ROI (Return on Influence) at these basic levels is limited. Short-term results do not encourage employees, clients, customers or suppliers. The result is they either lack complete understanding or they are not able to achieve long-term goals or objectives, grow in the areas of critical or creative thinking, assume leadership positions, and/or understand and contribute to the legacy of the organization.

In order to address – and cross – the Mission Critical Line on the Influence Pyramid, we have to be willing to share our own identity, and let others see how we are contributing to the legacy of the organization as well as to our individual legacies. In plain language: we need to "up our game" by elevating our messages!

And don't forget the often-overlooked side of influencing others in a more powerful and positive way – active listening. When we listen actively and intentionally to what others are sharing we have the opportunity to assist them in elevating their message. Asking questions or making encouraging comments allows you to learn more, support others more effectively, and create more sustainable influence. Use questions or statements like:

- Help me understand…
- Can you give me an example of…?
- That makes sense in terms of…

Use encouraging and supportive body language like:

- Leaning forward or tilting your head towards the speaker.
- Using an affirmative nod after a well-made point.
- Laughing or smiling appropriately.

When we listen attentively and actively, we are adding to the personal experience of that specific conversation or presentation.

The more we listen intentionally to others and speak in a way that reveals our personal experiences, the easier it is to create understanding, cooperation and collaboration.

THE PLOT BEHIND THE STORY

*"The stories we live and tell provide coherence
and meaning and orient our sense of purpose."*
– Sharon Daloz Parks

Let's go back and set the stage for the *Little Timmy* story. What events occurred before that young man raised his hand and told the story of *Little Timmy?*

The leadership team of this chemical manufacturing plant wanted to empower their front-line managers. They wanted them to be able to make changes without having to ask permission or be afraid of retribution. They wanted to foster more direct action by the managers, less "administrivia" for the senior management staff, and increased productivity while enhancing the bottom line.

Management decided to do this through harnessing the power of individual stories, and they asked me to conduct the session as one of a series of management development programs being held each month. Front-line managers from all areas of the plant attended the program, from the research and development scientists to the plant floor supervisors. It was an eclectic mix of ages, educational levels, ethnic groups, areas of expertise, and tenure within the organization. The groups were ninety percent male.

The session began like most others, with a story from my personal experience. In this instance, I shared a story about my son when he was 3 years old. As is often the case when a story is well told, you could have heard a pin drop as those in the room leaned forward, eager to hear the story.

Afterwards there was some discussion.

- "What made it a good story?"
- "Why did it hold people's interest?"

We also looked at additional foundational material about stories.

- "Why are stories important as a communication tool?"
- "How can stories be used?"
- "What is the structure of a story all about?"

We debriefed the story I shared about my son to help enhance the understanding of the process.

Next, I asked each participant to share one specific concept that needed to be communicated to his/her team during the course of that week. I told them I did not even need to necessarily understand the concept; however, the concept needed to be important and specific for each individual team. In other words, the general concept of "Teamwork is Good" was not the type of concept I wanted them to share. It needed to be specific to their respective areas of responsibility, and immediately necessary and practical for their employees.

As we went around the room, each participant shared a brief sentence.

"Now you have ten minutes to come up with a story to illustrate your point," I said. "It can be an experience from your childhood, about your kids, your parents, or grandparents. It can be about sports, about something here at the plant, or a story from some other job you may have had. The frame for your story is only limited by your experience or imagination."

The groans were good-natured. They were used to me (after all, I had my own hard hat and size 4 steel-toed boots – which drove the purchasing department nuts). I was considered part of the team, and they were always willing to participate. To help the process along, examples of several possible "story starters" were provided:

- When I was a child...
- Playing _____ taught me...
- On my very first job/project...
- The best boss I ever had...

As I listened to the chatter in the room, there were the usual couple of participants who were quite sure, in their own minds, they had no stories to tell. Funny, when I asked them to think about what they had done in the past 24 hours, they were soon crafting wonderful stories to share about children's soccer games, an incident during the early shift at the plant, and so on. Suddenly they were focused on appropriate, anecdotal narratives, and the "buzz" in the room began to emerge with excitement and positive energy.

After ten minutes I asked, "Who wants to volunteer first to share your story?"

The tall, handsome, young man with his "just chillin' attitude" – who always sat in the far left-hand corner of the room, his lanky frame stretched out in his chair – was the first to raise his hand. You could have knocked me over with a feather as he began in an almost hushed tone...

"It was three o'clock in the morning..."

THE STORY BEHIND THE PLOT

"The most important thing is to try and inspire people
so they can be great in whatsoever they want to do."
– Kobe Bryant

Back up even further before the *Little Timmy* story emerged. Visualize a group of people coming into the meeting room, gathering around the U-shaped table in small groups of 2, 3 or 4. The tension was becoming palpable; the "buzz" grew louder with each passing moment.

A special meeting had been called by the plant manager. Questions were being asked, assumptions and "what if" scenarios were being discussed. Everyone knew there was important information coming down the pike, and they dreaded the delivery.

Like other organizations in crisis, executives in the company headquarters, located in another state, imported someone from a totally different culture – a person who had been very successful in a similar situation – to "save the day." In this case, the plant manager was from "down under" (Australia) – definitely a different

39

part of the world. He often used unfamiliar colloquialisms and always spoke softer and faster than members of his staff, most of them having grown up in this place of both natural beauty and eccentric charm. It was the traditional South of the USA. Here in the South, conversation was slow and as smooth as good whiskey.

There had been a number of these meetings over several preceding months, and they were almost always less than successful. The communication lacked connection and by extension, it lacked positive influence. Now, here they were again, wondering what changes would be announced and what conflicts would arise because of potential misunderstandings.

The plant manager came into the room. As everyone sat down, the room quieted.

Beginning in his usual soft-spoken manner, he began a story of a personal experience early in his career. He described an environment and situation similar to the one that had generated all the "buzz" before he entered the room.

The leadership team, both executives and managers, was transfixed! Everyone was focused on the story as it began to unfold. Masterfully, he took the participants from the "then" of the story to the "now" of the current situation, drove home his point, and asked some simple questions:

- "How can we accomplish similar results here?"
- "What can we, as a team, do differently to turn things around at our plant?"

The answers that began forming in the minds throughout the room made it clear. The story provided the touchpoint necessary for everyone to be on the same page. The change was communicated, resolving potential conflicts before they appeared. The communication was genuine, and the connection was complete. There was a shift in power! The message had been elevated to cross the Mission Critical Line of the Influence Pyramid by using a personal experience in a strategic manner to communicate.

This example of providing personal insight from a similar experience led to greater influence and understanding. It was the result of a similar program I had conducted with the senior management team at the plant a few weeks before the story of *Little Timmy* emerged. The results from this earlier session were beginning to take effect. The senior management team saw those results and they were eager to expand the power of storytelling to the front-line supervisors – hence the session which provided an opportunity for the *Little Timmy* story to emerge.

Senior management realized that stories define the culture of every organization, and culture dictates behavior. People do things based on what is acceptable. What is acceptable is learned through the stories, both seen and heard, throughout the organization. The way to elevate your message to influence any kind of change within your team, organization, or community is by changing the stories, adding new ones, reframing old ones, and understanding and using the power of your personal stories to communicate, clarify, and influence the change desired.

The Leadership Team knew the front-line managers and super-visors needed to be coached in order to tell those stories well. They understood this because of their own personal experience with me in a similar workshop and subsequent coaching. A series of coaching sessions was scheduled for the supervisors and mid-management personnel to work with me. The stories were expanded to elevate the messages (points) to guarantee greater influence for changes that needed to be made.

ENGINEERING EPIPHANIES

"Gratitude bestows reverence, allowing us to encounter everyday epiphanies, those transcendent moments of awe that change forever how we experience life and the world."
– John Milton

We influence change when we make our processes and procedures come alive by using stories from our own experience.

- What portions of your journey are you sharing with your team?
- What epiphanies are you engineering as a leader?
- What insights have you shared that provide the opportunity for others to "get it?"

Engineering epiphanies (also known as AHA!! moments) are the essence of leadership and legacy – through stories, events, active listening, role modeling and mentoring. The power of your influence as a leader will increase, and your team will "get" the elevated message you send through your unique signals and the symbols you exhibit.

Increasingly, leaders who invest time and effort in learning how to craft and tell stories that engage, teach, and empower are having an easier time moving their teams and organizations to where they want and need them. This is the opposite of those leaders who keep presenting information in charts and graphs alone.

When leaders are as good at shaping, using, and telling stories as they are at collecting and analyzing data, they have a much easier time influencing the changes they envision throughout their organization.

Sometimes we do not think about the fact that every team or organization, any group or community, is composed of folks at different levels whom we are trying to influence. It is often easier to just tell someone (or an entire group) to "do" something than it is to elevate our message in order to maximize our ROI (Return on Influence).

THE RESULTS & UNDERLYING IMPORTANCE OF LITTLE TIMMY

"The stories we tell each other matter."
–Ava DuVernay

Influencing front-line managers to make changes independently – this was the goal of the management development program. The question was, at which level of influence should the leaders aim?

After a few of the stories had been shared, we took a break. Without asking permission, or even telling anyone else, several of the participants gathered together and decided to do something about *Little Timmy*. Before the end of the break, unbeknownst to me or the majority of the program participants, they placed a call and made arrangements to have *Little Timmy* removed from his home in the pond behind the plant.

Two days later, back in my office, I received four different emails all with the same picture – *Little Timmy* in the "pet taxi" going to a better place.

Realizing that empowerment had happened organically, senior management wanted to take advantage of these results, and an unexpected, internal marketing campaign began. Golf shirts, with an alligator embroidered above the company logo and *Timmy's Team* written below, were given to every manager and supervisor in the plant. Posters showing *Little Timmy* leaving the plant for a better place were commonplace. Everyone clearly understood that many common-sense changes could be made without specific permission or retribution.

This particular plant had been operating in crisis mode for several years. It had been bought and sold multiple times, productivity was down, quality was diminished, profits were non-existent, and the fear of imminent closure was an ever-present reality of life. Managers and staff alike were in a perpetual state of uncertainty concerning the stability and security of their jobs and their future.

As the story of *Little Timmy* cascaded throughout the plant it became a symbol for responsibility being accepted and change being made.

Did the story of *Little Timmy* save the plant? Certainly not by itself. However, the habit of sharing and teaching with stories of personal experience helped create a new culture of responsibility and empowerment. The bottom line is that after 5+ years, not only was the plant still open, but it was productive, profitable, and hundreds of people were still employed, contributing to the life of their community and ensuring the future of their families.

In this specific example of the *Little Timmy* story, it actually turned out to encompass all three of the personal experience story-types: It was PERSONAL because our young man described his own experience with *Little Timmy*. It was somewhat like a PARABLE in that the "lesson learned" showed up in the responsibility taken by the "empowered" individuals who made arrangements for *Little Timmy* to go to a better place. It definitely became a corporate LEGEND through the internal marketing plan and the retelling of the story to every new employee who joined the group as time moved forward.

THE CHALLENGE: SUSTAINABLE METHOD FOR BETTER COMMUNICATION & GREATER RETURN ON INFLUENCE

"Identity is a life story."
– Dan McAdams.

Is the story of *Little Timmy* a pipe dream in terms of the communication process in most organizations? This is a true story, and similar to several scenarios I've witnessed in other manufacturing plants, financial service organizations, hospitality companies, energy corporations, public utilities, and non-profits.

In my experience, leaders who want to elevate their message and communication processes use stories, as strategic and operational tools. To ensure that the stories will work, they must be believable, and the leader sharing them must absolutely believe in them. Whether it is a personal story, or repeated from a lesson learned possibly about someone else, or a corporate legend, a story well-crafted and well-told will capture the

47

listener's attention and communicate in a more universal way than the traditional data dump that is often used to announce things or to present necessary information. It's a great way to learn about the people within an organization, where they came from, what they believe, what they value, and how they want to be treated. The more we know about those we work with, the stronger our organizations become. Morale is higher, productivity increases, the sound of laughter and camaraderie is evident. It rings from the boardroom to the shop floor; from the executive offices to the front-line; from the most traditional, resistant, long-term manager who adheres to the "we've always done it this way" adage, to the young, techno-savvy kid who asks "why?" Synergy is greater; employees, customers, clients, and suppliers are happier. An atmosphere of growth and forward thinking is manifested. In a nutshell, employees become more engaged and more productive. Quite a "return on investment" for doing what comes naturally – telling the story well in order to elevate your message to maximize your "return on influence".

The "trick" (if there really is one) is that just because you use stories from your personal experiences to elevate your message, there is no guarantee you'll instantly have a greater return on your influence. You must be able to tell the story well!! And using stories must be a consistent methodology used throughout the organization.

Integrating stories as an operational methodology takes time, intent, and practice. While many of the stories may seem like "magic," in terms of the results that are manifested because of the story, they aren't "magic." Some are told only once. Others, like *Little Timmy*, become legendary within the organization.

Stories have been around forever, since the hunters and gatherers at the fire passed along information about where the best game was located. The parables from over 2000 years ago are still told and adapted for problem resolution, moral object lessons, correcting behavior and calming fears, etc. Through the years, and still today in many homes, the evening meal is the time when stories from work or school, business trips or holidays, plans for the future, events, and hobbies are shared. The information is passed on, questions may be generated and/or answered, and new ideas are formed or shared.

In today's business world there are a variety of digital platforms and social media sites – Facebook, LinkedIn, Twitter, YouTube videos, blogs, emails, and more that all provide multiple ways of sharing our stories. Everyone should have the opportunity to live a great story. Every organization has a story repeated through the products and/or services it provides (or doesn't). When those stories – whether personal or professional experiences, parables or organizational legends – are shared, we elevate our messages, expand our influence, and build our legacies because of the lives we touch through sharing.

While many of us are way too dependent on our phones for communication and information, we still have opportunities to elevate our messages through the experiences we live and the stories we share. Telling stories allows us to employ sound, tone, touch, body language, energy and excitement as we communicate and share beyond what we see on our screens. Yes, stories and storytelling are sustainable when we take the time to use them consistently for strategic and operational reasons. As with many things in this ever-changing technology-based world we live in… "use it or lose it." It is a choice!

THE WORLDWIDE PANDEMIC

"You are braver than you believe, and stronger than you seem, and smarter than you think."
– Christopher Robin

At the time this book is being written, our world is in the throes of the COVID-19 worldwide pandemic. Stories of death, sadness, recovery, and joy are heard every day. We wear masks, we self-isolate, we stay home, we work from home, we long for "normalcy," and we use technology to communicate in different and expanded ways. It is a challenging and difficult time in our world.

Not a day goes by that I have not thought or heard someone else wonder:

- "How long will this last?"
- "When will things be back to normal?"
- "Will things ever be the same again?"

My current belief is that whether this environment lasts for months or years, days or weeks, things will never be quite the same. Leaders have seen how work can be done remotely, and how the myriad of different ways of using technology can provide opportunities to connect. According to the current news we will be allowing more employees to continue to work remotely, or perhaps on staggered schedules, as things evolve to whatever the "new normal" will be.

Opportunities for up close and personal, face-to-face communication will gradually become a hybrid of the traditional 9 to 5 in the company office workplace and working remotely.

Whenever and in whatever way the future of work evolves going forward, there will be many stories to share about lessons learned through this unprecedented and challenging time. Visions and values may be changing; certainly, how we can communicate through, around, up, and over obstacles (some still unknown to us) may also require different techniques and strategies.

Those personal epiphanies and changes will need to be communicated – whether verbally, digitally, or visually – in a rapid and creative fashion, to ensure messages are elevated to higher standards and methodologies. Businesses are already pivoting to do things faster and differently than before. Influencing those with whom we work, the clients we serve, and the communities in which we participate, requires that we start now to elevate our messages; such positive influences are needed more today than ever before in our collective histories. What stories and epiphanies will you share from these challenging times?

A Case in Point: COVID-19 Patient Influenced by a Hospital Housekeeper

The man lay alone in his pressurized room at a hospital. He had a severe case of Covid-19, and it looked like he was losing the battle.

A priest came to administer last rites. The patient said goodbye to his family via FaceTime.

This is but another example of the necessary strict restrictions demanded by COVID-19. At this point, thousands of people around the world are forced to suffer and die alone, without family or friends nearby.

It is also why the medical teams depend heavily on non-medical personnel, such as housekeepers and custodians, to spend time with the patients, to lighten the mood and provide encouragement when patients have lost hope, by offering an attentive ear when patients need to process their emotions. They provide so much more than the traditional scope of an entry level job.

They are sometimes referred to as "invisible" workers. In reality, they provide a human link with patients whose primary contacts are members of the medical team who have rightly been hailed as the heroes and "sheroes" because of their heroic efforts during the pandemic.

The staff members who were in the various patient rooms every day to clean, received material from the hospital chaplain to help them interact with these seriously ill patients.

In this case a housekeeper, originally from Central America, and a retired armed forces colonel dealing with the illness, met in the colonel's pressurized hospital room, where he faced death. They started by talking about the weather and other small talk. And through these daily conversations, the housekeeper began to encourage the patient not to give up hope; she encouraged him to fight for his life.

Soon their conversations were more about sharing their identities with each other rather than talking only about his health and how bad his prognosis seemed to be. Gradually they began to share information about their children and their faith.

His reaction was one of amazement that the housekeeper was not scared to be close to him. She in turn, felt sorry for him, being apart from his family while in such pain. She commented, "I wanted to make sure that he knew he was not alone."

Even though there was somewhat of a language barrier, as English was not the housekeeper's first language, they quickly formed a bond. "When a patient is treated with compassion and love, language is not a barrier," the housekeeper explained. This mindset of compassion and understanding represents how important and vital the work of these typically entry-level staff members really is in the bigger picture. Because there are strict limits imposed on visits from family and even chaplains, the housekeepers and custodians are often able to provide emotional support to the patients and their families. It is a scary position because these "invisible" workers are often caught between their own economic hardship and the deadly disease.

These small moments of comfort can save lives. According to Jane Dutton, a scholar at the University of Michigan, "It only takes 40 seconds of caring interaction to change a patient in a way that affects their whole health trajectory."

I guarantee you that these housekeepers and custodians have never heard of the Influence Pyramid. Yet, as they move beyond small talk about the weather or other everyday things to forge a bond with a patient facing death by sharing their own identity, amazing things can happen. Their daily interactions elevate their messages and they are finally being recognized by hospital executives as playing a much greater role than their job description requires.

The happy ending to this particular case was that the colonel didn't die. He improved enough to return home to his family with gratitude for a housekeeper whose influence played a very important role in saving his life.

His message after he left the hospital was, "I would just love to see her again and say thank you. People do not realize that in their brief engagements with other people, the words you say matter. And in the situation I was in, they really matter."*

Paraphrased from a recent article found at CNN's website (by Daniel Burke, CNN Religion Editor. June 11, 2020)

NOT GOING BY THE BOOK
A PUBLISHING COMPANY'S APPROACH

"I don't go by the rule book. I lead from the heart, not the head."
– Princess Diana

There are hundreds of examples in organizations around the planet that exemplify how leaders have elevated their message through personal stories to maximize their influence to change both behaviors and thought processes.

The CEO of a mid-size assessment and publishing company had great news to deliver concerning the phenomenal growth of the company over the past couple of years. It required recognition of the collective performance of the entire organization. It was also the precursor to the realization that the organizational structure was no longer appropriate. A "reorg" was in the making. The traditional methodology for this kind of communication in this company was a town hall meeting. Following tradition, an announcement for a company-wide town hall meeting was sent to all employees in every department.

The initial response was predictable.

"Not again!"

Over the previous 5 to 6 years, many organizational changes had been implemented. Objectively and certainly with hindsight, it was easy to understand that these changes had been good and right for the company, a testament to its continuing growth and success.

Often, town hall meetings designed to announce changes are not easy. The larger the organization, the more difficult it is to frame the message, the greater the chance for miscommunication and misunderstanding.

This particular CEO had additional challenges. He had only been part of the organization for 2 years, and despite the tremendous growth and success in size, margins, and service occurring on his "watch," he was still considered an outsider – the "new guy."

He realized this opportunity to communicate and influence every member of the staff could work for him or against him – for the future of the organization or against it. He understood that his best chance of exerting a positive influence on every-one – regardless of who they were, how long they'd been with the company, or how skeptical or afraid they might be of the potential announcement's effect on them personally – was through elevating his message to come from above the "Mission Critical Line" of the Influence Pyramid.

Sharing his personal journey from early in his career to his current position, he detailed his career path and also chose to reveal his feelings about the various moves he had made. He explained the changes in his responsibility, the difficult conversations with his wife, the impact on their relation-ship made with every change and move, and ultimately how his family's ability to function through all the changes was challenging at best, depending on the ages of his children, and the friends and/or family who would be left behind.

Moving forward on his selected career path was never easy. It was always a challenge to balance the demands of his career with the needs and wants of his family.

In every family that moves around a lot, especially during the children's formative years, there are a variety of reactions and attitudes that come to the surface, with each new place called home. Some welcome the opportunity and "adventure" of going to a new place, making new friends, seeing, learning, and/ or experiencing new things. Others are sad or angry at having to "start over" once again, in a new town, new school, making new friends, and trying to "fit in" in a new environment and possibly a new culture. And of course, this did not just apply to the children. Both the parents had similar thoughts about moving again, depending on how long they'd been in a certain place, how comfortable they were in their respective jobs, and what they were trying to achieve through accepting new career challenges and opportunities.

I can tell you from my own growing up years about being the "new girl," because we moved a great deal. I went to ten schools in twelve years. Sometimes I was eager to move and more often I did not want to leave my friends or be the "new girl" yet again. No, my dad was not in the military. He was a minister whose strength was taking small congregations and growing them to a larger church with a more positive influence in the community. Maybe he just had a short sermon file or, as one of my sister's used to say, "Daddy had an itchin' foot and blamed it on the Lord." The results of all those moves (and many more as an adult) are that I make friends easily, I love to travel, and I don't have a "hometown" to miss or return to, depending on my perspective. Truthfully, I grew up thinking it was normal to move a lot. As I grew older, I realized that not everyone moved as frequently as our family did.

My supposition is that the experiences of this CEO's children may have been similar to mine.

Perhaps that is why this particular CEO didn't hold anything back in terms of sharing some of these previous experiences and the challenges that every step (whether forward or backward) entailed. However, by being open, honest, sincere, and genuinely transparent, every person in the room identified with his personal journey. The story of change and its effects was based on a universal truth. Members of his leadership team, each staff member, and even the newest, entry-level hire understood that change affects everyone and that no one is alone in the experience.

This epiphany was engineered by a leader using wisdom, insight, and a genuine understanding of what resonates within the heart of every organization. It is important to remember that the heart of any organization is its people, and hearts are reached, touched, and ultimately influenced by its leaders elevating their messages and the delivery methodologies of those messages through their personal stories.

In terms of the Influence Pyramid – and because of the diversity of his staff, represented in terms of length of service, education, and cultures – the CEO realized he needed to influence across the levels of the Influence Pyramid. To reach everyone in the room, his best chance was to focus his message above the Mission Critical Line on the Leadership and Visionary Levels of the Pyramid. In this case he was not giving direction. He was creating buy-in while influencing the understanding of his audience. Challenges of this type are often faced by everyone at some point during their participation in the workforce. He also wanted to encourage those who heard his message to influence others to embrace and understand the changes that were coming in the weeks ahead. Of course, there were those who experienced anger and sadness, and others who welcomed the challenge and the opportunity to do something new and different. Truth be told, there were a bunch of employees somewhere in between those two mindsets. Yet the CEO understood that without sharing portions of his own journey and identity with them, understanding and cooperation would not be reached, and he would forever and always be known as the "hatchet man" – the "new guy" who came in and fired people!

Fortunately for the organization, he chose a more positive and deliberate way to influence everyone, those who would be laid off as well as those who would stay. It wasn't easy, but by elevating his message through the power of sharing his personal identity/story, his success rate was higher, many of his employees' perspectives changed, and the organization was able to move forward to achieve even greater things over the next several years. Those who left had a totally different view of the "reorg" process than the traditional "you wouldn't believe what they did to me today" attitude. Instead, they adapted some of the tips and strategies shared by the CEO to their own lives and were more positive about looking for new and different opportunities.

THE MAKING OF A CEO

"Leadership is influence, nothing more and nothing less."
– John C. Maxwell

Relatively new in the credit union industry, I was also very new to the "world of business." I had started my professional career as a schoolteacher. After 15 years in the education business, I knew it was time for me to "graduate."

Challenge number one was how to write a resume that would relate to the business world. It was hard, because including things like "I can teach," "I have been responsible for a class of 30 kids, some motivated and others not so much," and similar kinds of statements didn't sound very impressive to me, in a business context. Eventually, I was able to state things in "business-speak," and I began to apply for jobs to be able to contribute in a positive way.

As often happens in life, just when you least expect things... they "magically" happen. I went to an interview at the Hawaii Credit Union League (HCUL), the trade association for all the credit unions in the State of Hawaii, where I lived. I knew what a credit union was, because as a teacher I had belonged to a teacher's credit union. I had no idea what a trade association was, or what the people who worked for one actually "did."

I got the job – totally unprepared to do anything listed on the job description. They gave me a ton of manuals and binders to read so that I could become an expert on the subject during the 2 weeks prior to year-end. It was the holidays; who had time to read a 4-foot-high stack of manuals?

Apparently, I did! In between holiday activities and being a wife and a mom, I plunged into those manuals and reports for my first day on January 4, praying that there would NOT be a test!!

For about eighteen months I worked for HCUL and loved every minute of it. One of the projects I was assigned to work on was to find solutions for the credit unions who wanted to provide ATM (Automated Teller Machine) services for their members. During that project we identified several options, and it was determined that a separate organization was needed to make any of those options a reality. Very quickly Hawaii CU-ATM, Inc. was formed, along with a board of directors made up of several CEOs from some of the larger credit unions in the state. I was asked to be the CEO of this brand-new start-up.

And so, it began, with none of us realizing just how this organization would continue to evolve. The original thinking was that it would be primarily a "paper organization" and once we had a critical mass in terms of shareholder credit unions, those credit unions would choose whether or not they wanted an ATM on their premises. Then negotiations needed to be completed with one or two established ATM networks, ATM debit cards would be issued, and it would "magically" run itself. As the CEO, I was tasked to head up all those initiatives and report to the board periodically.

Now, at the time, I actually thought that there was a very small man who lived inside the ATM, and if he liked you, he would return your card and give you the requested amount of cash; if he didn't like you, he kept your money and your card! Well, maybe I did not actually think that. The truth is, I was pretty clueless as to the details of all these parts, having never been involved at a deep level with any of it.

This was my full-time business-related job, and I needed to address it and get it going. In fairly short order I was up to speed, but I still felt way out of my element. Then I began making appointments with credit unions for presentations to their respective boards, and to convince them to become shareholders in the corporation. Over the next few months, we signed up 25 credit unions as shareholders and users of the services (there were only about 90 credit unions in Hawaii at the time, and many of them were small organizations which didn't offer much more than savings and loans).

At the same time, I started negotiations with a regional ATM Network as well as a National Network. We signed all the appropriate documents with both networks, after a lot of learning on my part and multiple meetings over several months. I helped install ATMs, trained staff on how to market the program and how to support the machines in their daily operation. Suddenly (after a couple of years putting all the pieces together) we were ready to go live; and I was thinking, the corporation would just exist and run like clockwork.

Another false assumption, as we now became a back-office support organization for the shareholders; evolving meant that I was to continue marketing to sign up additional Credit Unions as shareholders, as well as hire and train staff to be the back-office machine, so to speak.

Instead of the organization being a paper corporation that worked "magically," there were now employees and we were busier than ever. I finally asked my board, "Why did you hire me for this position?" I had no experience except the brief research I had done before the corporation was established. It made no sense to me!

The chairman of my board was a long-time credit union CEO. She was both my mentor and my role model. She looked at me with a wry little smile and said, "We figured we could hire anyone to learn the technical things necessary, because we were all pretty much in the same boat in that regard. What we had neither the time nor patience for was to find someone with good people skills who could actually work with a variety of egos, i.e. the various credit unions CEOs."

I was stunned at her insight and her transparency and I was totally unprepared for the fact that they all believed in me so completely.

In terms of our Influence Pyramid, every one of those amazing CEOs making up the seven-member board, all knew that in order to bring me on board, they had to present the opportunity to me in an elevated manner; doing so would demonstrate their belief in me, as well as in the future of the brand new corporation. They started at the Leadership Level with me, telling me of their own experiences in starting a variety of different programs in their individual credit unions; they made sure to include both the things that worked easily, and the things that didn't. As I listened to the stories from their varied experiences, they resonated with me, and instilled enough confidence in me that I knew I wanted to try.

As time went by, they switched their level of influence to Visionary because they knew I was ready for new challenges and I wanted to contribute to the legacy of the corporation.

We had been in business just over 3 years, gone live on 2 different networks, completed our original 5-year plan in those first 3 years, paid a user fee reimbursement and successfully showed a return on the shareholders' investment. I had grown as a professional, as a leader, and I had learned from some of the best CEOs in the business.

A larger financial support corporation was interested in a merger with us. The board thought this was an excellent opportunity, and I was all for it. So, I learned how to lead a successful merger process.

I could have stayed after the merger, but I was eager to move on. With the boards blessing, I resigned and started my own business, speaking, training, and consulting for various financial organizations. As my business grew, I looked back and was often in awe of what we had done with nothing more than a small idea.

My focus changed slightly, and all the mentoring and challenging that I received during those 4 years is still paying off. I'm sure I was influenced by a variety of peripheral players during those years, and I've remained grateful for the trust those board members put in me, and for the way they elevated their messages to inspire and guide me, and celebrate all that we had accomplished together.

FALLING THROUGH THE CRACKS
AN EXAMPLE OF A POWERFUL AND HUMOROUS VISUAL STORY

"Mix a little foolishness with your serious plan;
it's lovely to be silly at the right moment."
– Anonymous

The CEO of a medium-sized credit union stood at the door-way between her office and the main lobby. Shaking her head in frustration, she realized that things could not be much more chaotic. The lobby was crowded, the volume level was high, as members navigated their way through a major lobby renovation. It was not pretty from any angle. People were complaining while tellers were trying to provide their normal level of friendly, helpful service. However, instead they found themselves spending more time apologizing for the disruption and providing explanations about how long the renovations would last.

The CEO and her staff had done all the "right" things in trying to prepare for these conditions. They had provided personal, printed, and electronic information to all the credit union members, explaining the rationale and necessity for the renovations, the time frame expected, and alternative branches, telephone contacts, and/or ATMs that could be used instead of coming into the main branch. Additionally, they had re-routed the teller lines to take advantage of the least affected areas in the lobby. They made light snacks and cold beverages available while members waited. They re-organized and re-located the kids' corner, so the children who accompanied their parents would not be in harm's way – all great things to do.

Yet, as often happens during a major renovation project being completed during regular business hours, things were a bit chaotic and definitely dusty.

"What else can we do? There has to be something that will alleviate the tension and frustration," the CEO thought.

Later that day she sent an email to each staff member, asking them to stay a few extra minutes, if possible, for a brief discussion. Although it was not a mandatory meeting, everyone stayed, attesting to the fact that this was a shared concern. After some "venting," frustrations were put aside and the discussion became more focused, trying to answer the question, "What else can we do?"

The obvious hurdle to overcome was that the situation was not going away until the renovation was complete. Finally, they decided that since the renovation was totally under the control of the contractor, the best they could do was something to make people smile and perhaps even laugh a bit to ease the tension. As the discussion continued, they collectively came up with a unique solution, and with the CEO's enthusiastic approval, the staff "built" their idea.

The visual created by the staff changed the entire atmosphere. They fashioned a pair of legs, in workman's clothing and work boots, and hung it through a hole in the lobby ceiling.

It was immediately noticeable by anyone who came into the lobby, causing lots of speculation and then laughter as folks realized it was just a dummy, emphasizing that the staff had not lost their sense of humor. They were doing their best to provide their normal, friendly atmosphere and excellent service during a challenging and difficult time.

When we compare how the CEO influenced her staff to understand how the unique, visual solution influenced the members coming and going through the lobby during the renovation process, we can see that both the CEO and the staff elevated their message (no pun intended). Both the CEO and the staff started at the Buy-in level of the Influence Pyramid.

They definitely had "buy-in" to start with because they knew they needed to do something to alleviate the frustration and tension their members were experiencing. However, they crossed the Mission Critical Line when they started sharing and contributing their own ideas, based on their own personal experiences and identities, and collectively their message was elevated. In this case, it was actually elevated in a literal sense as well, as they hung their "dummy legs" through a hole in the ceiling.

INTRODUCING A NEW SALES PROGRAM

---

*"Great sales people are relationship builders
who provide value and help their customers win."*
– Jeffrey Gitomer

As a freelance contractor, my program partner and I were tasked with introducing a new incentive program for front desk associates in hotels around the world.

The program was based on an incentive scale allowing the associates to earn extra money based on how many guests upgraded their reservations at check-in plus a percentage of the actual upgrade revenue generated. As an example, the guest was given options to stay in a suite or on a higher floor with a better view, or in a larger room with access to the hotel's club lounge, or a variety of other options, depending on the property. The hotel made extra profit based on an additional incremental rate for a room or suite that would otherwise have remained empty, earning them nothing. As facilitators we received a monthly percentage of the extra revenue each hotel generated. A simple program providing benefits for all concerned, the hotel guests, the associates, the hotel, and the facilitators.

The program was straightforward, based on simple questions and/or suggestions made by the associate. This was NOT a high-pressure approach, just the offer of a simple choice – an extension of good service. Our challenge was to encourage associates while asking them to do yet one more thing, efficiently, and with enthusiasm during the already sometimes lengthy check-in process.

The incentive of extra income for the associates was obvious, yet for some it did not really resonate. We realized that we needed to elevate the message to not only get buy-in to the program by all the front desk associates, but to share real-life stories that would resonate and allow them to identify with and be the leaders of the program. We chose to share quick stories of other associates from different properties who were successful in the program. With their permission, we showed their pictures as part of the PowerPoint presentation and explained what they were able to do with the extra money because of the personal goals they had established for themselves.

The realization was like seeing the proverbial light bulb turn on. Suddenly, these were real people, with real names, who worked at real hotels just like they did. Once in a while, someone would actually know one of these folks we used as examples, either because they used to work at that hotel or because they worked with the person at a different hotel at some point along the way. They realized that the quick personal stories we shared were about people who got up and went to work every day, just like the participants in the session. The brief personal stories resonated much more quickly than the more traditional "You need to set a goal to be successful" speech.

These were not our own personal stories or identities that we shared. But because we used, with permission, the pictures and stories of these other associates, we elevated our message to encourage and influence both ownership of the program and leadership internally at every front desk. It was definitely a domino effect, because once "ownership" was established, "leadership" within the program was evident. More associates earned more money by offering great choices. As facilitators we had access to more success stories to share with other properties, and the entire program grew across the brand in an organic manner.

ASK NOT WHAT THE COMPANY CAN DO FOR YOU; ASK WHAT YOU CAN DO FOR THE COMPANY

"It doesn't make sense to hire smart people and then tell them what to do; we hire smart people so they can tell us what to do."
– Steve Jobs

What about recruiting? The very best recruiters are storytellers. The reality is whichever organization and/or interviewee has the best story, wins.

Traditionally during the interview process, prospective employees are told all about the organization. In return the potential employee is expected to sell him/herself by answering a set of structured questions. What if the interview process was reversed? What if the interviewer did the selling?

When selling a company, a specific location, the job, and/or yourself, what better way to accomplish that than by using story, i.e. the story of your organization and the parts of your personal individual story that have contributed to the organizational story. Your questions for the candidate can then be built on and reference how the candidate may fit into the organization based on what you have shared. And the question can be simply put, "Tell me how you think you will best fit into our organization?" The clues to the strength of your story will be in how well your candidate uses that specific information in responding. The bottom line is that those who paint the most compelling word picture of the organization, it's vision and values, will get the candidates of choice because the message has been elevated to influence toward Buy-in, Leadership and in some cases Visionary, depending on the position for which the interviewee is being interviewed.

While every interviewer may not feel comfortable (at first) using the storytelling approach, using story starters such as:

- When I first started with this company...
- Working on the team that...
- My first/current boss at this company taught me...

should definitely be helpful as the interviewer prepares for the interview. In most cases, sharing experiences provides much better insight into how a prospective employee may fit in the organization. It is definitely a more interactive approach than the standard, dare I say "rote" demands often made during the interview process, i.e. "Provide a service-driven example of when you successfully aided a customer." While this is not a bad thing to do, interviewees who have been interviewed by a number of different organizations using a similar approach, will develop their own standard "rote" answers.

Admittedly, different styles of communication work for different people. Using experiences, stories and/or anecdotes during the interview process is another option that can give an organization a different perspective of their candidates. One suggestion is to have several different individual interviewers for each candidate, using different styles and methodologies. You may be surprised how the quality of your candidates "shows up" when results of the interviews are compared. Yes, this practice may take a little longer than either one individual interviewing or even a panel interview process. Like any change or new way of thinking about or doing something, it can and should be modified to fit the specific organization; over time, it becomes easier and much more informative.

- What are the compelling pieces of your corporate/organizational story?
- Your history?
- Your philosophy?
- Your values?
- Your vision?
- Your mission/purpose?
- Your progress?
- Your "lessons learned?"
- Your achievements?
- How you feel about your people?
- How do your people (really) feel about your organization?
- Customer/Client result stories.
- Product stories.

How many of the stories are "legendary?"

The list can go on and on. Ask your team and listen to what is being said in the hallways, break room, and parking lot about your organization. Do not forget that in our "current normal" way of working remotely because of COVID-19, you should also check the chat box of your virtual meetings. You may be surprised at what is being said. With this information:

- Pick four or five of the most compelling points embedded in your corporate story.
- Refine them.
- Share them with your candidates of choice during the interview process.

Please do not consider these specific suggestions as "silver bullets" in terms of perfecting your interview process. They are provided as options that deserve exploration as well as consideration.

Remember, especially during the interview process, we are dealing with individuals who are all different and have different approaches to work, understandings of workplace culture, language, communication, and ethics. When dealing with people, one size does NOT fit all. In my experience, if we get things right between 85% and 95% of the time in terms of the people we hire and work with, we are doing a GREAT job!!

Here is what experience and observation have proved to me over the course of my professional life. Elevating your message during the interview process is critical to elevating the quality and "fit" of the people you hire. As you elevate your message to address the Leadership and Visionary Levels, you will have a more creative and independent workforce that does not need to be constantly supervised or micromanaged. Therefore, this process does not just apply to their education or experience levels. It can actually improve the "fit" of a given candidate with the rest of the team already in place.

Since many employees have been working at home during the pandemic, more organizations will move forward with more employees working from home than ever before. This is another reason to determine, via the recruiting process, how productive a candidate may be working from home in the post-pandemic world.

Would spending less time supervising and more time collaborating on and/or creating new ideas and methodologies to advance your organization faster, ensure more productivity as well as profit? Would it be something of value? If so, consider different ways you can elevate your message.

PERSONALITY IS THE BRAND

"Personality begins where comparison leaves off.
Be unique. Be memorable. Be confident. Be proud."
– Shannon L .Alder

How are the compelling pieces of our corporate/organizational story embodied in our brand? Ultimately the personality of your organization is the brand. I believe organizations, divisions, departments, or branches develop personalities just like people do. Listening to the way individuals talk about suppliers, customers, or other divisions within an organization, the words used to describe them are the same words used to describe people.

One may be talking about a client organization and comment, "They are great people to deal with." They are easy going, or cooperative, or helpful, or very professional, or quite thorough, or fun to deal with. On the other hand, another organization might be described as aggressive, condescending, difficult, un-ethical, nitpicking, or humorless.

This is remarkable when you think about it. Often an organization represents hundreds, if not thousands of people and yet it is described as if it were an individual. I believe all organizations have personalities. What is happening now is that the personality – what they are actually like to deal with, on a day-to-day basis – is, de facto becoming the brand.

It does not matter what advertising, public relations, or corporate communications may say. What an organization is really like to deal with, decision-by-decision, interaction-by-interaction, day-in and day-out – in other words, the personality of the unit is becoming the brand!

There are four, interrelated things leaders need to understand about branding in today's environment:

1. You do not own your brand.
2. The conversation in the marketplace owns your brand.
3. You cannot control that conversation.
4. You can only participate in the conversation.

This has always been true to some degree. What is happening now is the conversation is so widespread and happens so quickly, that it is even more true today than it has ever been.

When that conversation, in what I call the "omniblog" – all the various ezines, blogs, networking sites, bulletin boards, "twitterings," and other social media – reaches any kind of consensus, it defines your brand for your marketplace. The challenge for organizations, and especially their leaders, is to locate and then participate in these conversations.

Leading organizations today have people whose job and purpose is to monitor that conversation in the "omniblog," and then contribute to it or disseminate it internally for others to act on. This allows them to be aware of what the market is saying and gives them an opportunity to influence – not control – how conversation evolves.

To some, at first glance, this will look like another one of those "airy-fairy, fuzzy, consultant-theory-type things." It is NOT. This is a serious, hard business reality in today's marketplace.

Several years ago, a major computer manufacturer decided to cut costs by cutting and outsourcing much of their tech support. This tangibly reduced the availability of personnel to respond to customer enquiries. In short order, a couple of influential bloggers started writing about this change in the way they were doing business.

Within a few months the tom-toms beating out in cyberspace created a major customer backlash that was eventually picked up by mainstream media. The end result: their stock price was hammered by over 20%; they were forced to take dramatic action after all the "mea culpas." The point: they did not pick up this smoldering grass fire quickly enough to respond before it became such a major conflagration.

Many executives might struggle with the concept of defining "personality" to the marketplace – but none of them have any difficulty understanding "the stock dropped 20%!"

Another well-known organization that has taken personality branding to the extreme is the Virgin group of companies, led by Richard Branson. Some may argue that Branson and his Virgin corporation have become as much a branding machine as an operating company. The Virgin logo is on a tremendously diverse series of businesses around the world. From bookstores to airlines, to soda pop, to health club services, to mobile phone services, to internet services. Just about the only thing this collection of businesses has in common is the Virgin label.

The remarkable thing to me is the consistency with which these businesses have adopted the personality branding philosophy. Whether you are talking about a health club in South Africa, a mobile phone service in Australia, or a retail store in Toronto, these organizations have a philosophy of doing business and an attitude toward life that is remarkably similar across cultures, continents, and companies.

How does an organization's personality show through? Several years ago, my late husband (Warren Evans), was in the Coolangotta Airport in Australia to fly a Virgin Blue Airline flight to Sydney. After going through all the security procedures, he stopped and took some photographs of one of the familiar sites in any airport, the carry-on luggage-sizing device. Almost everywhere around the world, huge signs full of warnings and diagrams about weight and dimensions sit atop these things.

The Virgin Blue station had three different carry-on sizing devices, also with great big signs. The first one said, "You can have a huge ego, but only a bag this size."

The next one said, "All the emotional baggage you want, as long as it fits in here."

The third one, in great big letters, simply said, "Size Really Does Matter."

That is a great example of an organization exhibiting parts of its personality that differentiates it from everyone else.

What is the leadership lesson for everyone who influences the way an organization exhibits its personality? I am pretty sure that Richard Branson did not get into one of his planes and fly to the Coolangotta Airport in Australia and write the script for the carry-on luggage-sizers. Yet the staff at Virgin Blue obviously "gets it." They understand what the company is about and the personality they are trying to project to their customers. By using aspects of that personality via marketing materials, events, techniques and strategies, external messages to their customers and suppliers have been elevated because they have shared their identity that is totally integrated by the personality of their leader.

This is not to encourage all leaders to aspire to a specific personality as expressed by those leaders who "get it." Rather, it is a reminder of the importance of the organization's personality that becomes their brand. Again, the message is elevated to influence at the Leadership level, above the Mission Critical line of our Influence Pyramid, both internally and externally, via what has become a "Legendary" personality!

There are dozens of other examples of organizations, both large and small, that understand and integrate the personality is the brand philosophy.

During an election campaign, I drove by a truck that pumps out septic tanks. On the back was a sign that said, "Warning: may be carrying political promises."

It made me smile.

- When is the last time your organization did something that made everyone smile?
- How are you elevating your message in ways that provide you with an opportunity to influence the conversation in the marketplace about the personality of your brand?*

*The contents of this chapter are used with permission, copied and adapted from a similar chapter in The Future, by Warren Evans Copyright © 2009, Warren Evans Ideas, Inc.

THERE'S ALWAYS A COST
WHAT IS THE COST OF NOT ELEVATING
YOUR MESSAGE APPROPRIATELY?

"Because teachers are like messengers,
they carry an elevating message."
– Nanoosha Nany

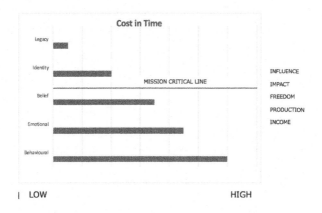

This chart shows the amount of time that a leader typically has to invest in terms of trying to influence and have a positive impact at the various levels of the Influence Pyramid. The less independent or creative thinking and/or decision-making that is done by the person being influenced, the more time and the more costly it is to the leader. The reality of this cost to the leader/organization to NOT elevate their messages is that the leader spends more time being a supervisor or a manager, and has less time or freedom to spend on enhancing the vision and expanding the strategies necessary for success.

WHY is this Important?

Many in leadership positions spend a great deal of time using messages that basically provide a road map that helps people get from point A to point B to point C and on and on. It is relatively easy to do, makes giving instructions/directions easy and often seems like it doesn't take much time. However, as our Cost Model shows, it often takes more time and costs more than expected.

Another consequence of spending more, rather than less time on this type of communication is that it gives, at the most, limited empowerment to those the leader is trying to influence. Yes, you may eventually get buy-in to the organizational vision, values, mission and direction for the future. In many cases, that is enough.

However, when we take a step back and look at the longer term and vision for the future of the company, going from A to B is a very short-term result. In my experience as a leader and consultant/coach to others in leadership positions, the best accomplishment usually attained with this approach is that the leader becomes a micro-manager of minutia and "administrivia." This is a pretty obvious clue there is a problem in moving the organization and employees, customers/clients, or suppliers forward. When we return to our Cost Model it becomes apparent that the primary motivators for most leaders would be to have:

- Greater influence.
- Greater impact.
- Greater freedom.

in terms of time, and ultimately

- More productivity and profit.

These five things: influence, impact, freedom, productivity, and profit, are the primary motivators for most people in leadership positions. They want all those things to improve throughout their team and/or organization. However, "wanting" things to happen is part of the overall problem.

Our Mission Critical Line on the Influence Pyramid stands out even more in terms of inspiring others to be motivated through the enhancement of these five basic motivators. When the majority of our time is spent giving directions, micro-managing, and struggling to get buy-in to the vision, goals, and objectives, we are at best maintaining the status quo.

How does one move from the status quo to more growth, better service, greater profit margins, and the plain old enjoyment of who you are and what you do every day? It is often an elusive answer, only because it's relatively simple, yet perceived as more difficult than it should be.

The following examples are from leaders I have worked with over the years; they show how these leaders have crossed the Mission Critical Line in influencing their employees, customers/clients, colleagues, and suppliers.

As we learned from the *Little Timmy* example, through work-shops, coaching, and ultimately being consistent in sharing relevant experiences, leaders at all levels – in organizations small and large, national and international – have shown that with effort and a willingness to be a bit vulnerable, progress begins. Productivity and profitability follow as the practice of sharing increases, empowerment grows, and ultimately more people ENJOY their work and the shared possibilities this creates.

FROM GRIEF TO GRATITUDE ;
THE CHALLENGE OF DEALING
WITH LOSS

"If the only prayer we ever said was 'thank you',
that would be enough."
– Meister Eckhart

It reminds me of the story of a CEO of a small, university-based credit union. She experienced an unexpected personal heartbreak, losing a loved one in a tragic accident. Part of the recovery process centered around her going back to work. Typical of a small organization, her staff and many of their members were like family. To her it seemed that every member who came into the credit union felt compelled to step into her office, offer personal condolences, and give her a comforting hug during their credit union visits.

She felt this was important for the staff and the credit union members, and she endured the well-meaning hugs. "I've never felt so well-hugged in my life," she remarked in a tired voice. As we talked, I realized that her members were not allowing her to grieve. With each person who came to give her a hug, she was reliving the painful moments all over again.

"You need to let your staff help you be less accessible for a while," I said.

"How do I explain that while I appreciate the thoughts and hugs, I am having a difficult time dealing with the pain?" she questioned.

I suggested that she present her dilemma to her staff and ask them to work together to protect her from having to deal directly with the members during a specific time frame each day. She could choose to be in the building or not. Involving her team by simply relating at least a portion of her grieving story and process would give them permission to work together. After all, when you access the collective imagination and experience of a collaborative team, anything is possible.

Their response was both supportive and enthusiastic. They encouraged her to do whatever she felt would best serve her needs during the designated time frame each day. All sorts of ideas emerged – arranging to see her therapist during the specific time frame one day each week, go shopping away from the credit union location, treating herself to a spa treatment, catching up on her reading, spending time at a nearby park to just be, as well as many other suggestions. Eventually a regular routine was established. After about a month the visits by well-meaning members were dramatically reduced.

The CEO had time to pursue other opportunities as a distraction or to just relax and reflect. Certainly, this helped the CEO with the grieving process. The "bonus" was that through her staff working with her to make this happen, they became a more solid and collaborative team in all areas of their responsibilities. Why? Because they shared their own stories, while becoming part of her recovery story. Good storytelling is the "magic" in building better teams. Exchanging personal stories encourages a sense of belonging and leads to influencing above the Mission Critical Line on the Influence Pyramid. By influencing at the Leadership Level sometimes the most surprising team member will emerge as a leader. When influencing at the Visionary Level it encourages those who are influenced to influence others.

CHANGING THE PRESENTATION METHODOLOGY

"There's power in allowing yourself to be known and heard,
in owning your own story, in using your authentic voice."
– Michelle Obama

Another company conference; another company logo bag and golf shirt; another endless PowerPoint presentation of statistics about the past year's productivity and next year's goals. What creative geniuses were at work planning this?

Yet how many of us have been to professional conferences, organizational meetings, or company events over and over, where the format rarely changes, even in virtual meetings? Some of us, the optimists in the crowd, are ever hopeful that this year, this meeting, this conference, will be different. This year the CEO will do more than read his/her remarks. The CFO will not read his/her slides. And just maybe this year, less than half the presentations will not start with the words, "I know you can't see this in the back…"

Isn't it strange that many MBA programs manage to do a fine job of dehumanizing the communication skills of their graduates? They preach the doctrine of the almighty spreadsheet as a communication tool. While it may be a handy thing for calculating the traditional ROI (Return on Investment), it is surely one of the least effective tools in the world for leading people and elevating your message to gain a better ROI (Return on Influence). And then we wonder why the "troops" do not rally to the cause?

This year was no different. The CFO of this state's department of transportation had prepared slides with all kinds of stats, comparison charts, numbers of roads completed or repaired, and so on. But the department director took another approach.

Deciding to focus on having pride in work accomplished, he related a story that he had been told about Nikita Khrushchev's first visit to the United States. Whether the story was related exactly as it happened is not the point of the story. The point is how the story was used to elevate the employees' understanding, to influence the development of a sense of pride in accomplishment, and to generate a vision of the possibilities going forward.

The story is told that after having been shown New York, and Washington D.C., then flown to Los Angeles to experience Disneyland, Khrushchev was asked which of the technological and engineering marvels he had seen impressed him the most. His immediate response was "the interstate highway system," which he had observed from his window seat on the plane while flying across the country.

The Director went on to talk about how the highway system in their state, and throughout the country, was truly the backbone of the nation. The economy would come to an abrupt standstill without the highways; children could not get to school; adults couldn't get to work; friends and families couldn't easily travel from one town to the next to visit each other. Without the efforts of each and every person in that department, each and every day, the state could not function. Pride in what they were accomplishing, and the understanding that they were really part of something much bigger than their individual jobs, suddenly became real.

Why did that inspire members of the department? The director told the story and related it to their personal work situation. He used the story as a foundation piece, built on it, and held his audience in the palm of his hand because they were connected emotionally.

There was no PowerPoint during the story.

Was his influence felt? Did behavior change? Was morale given a shot in the arm? Did pride in their daily contribution to the goals of the department become more apparent? Absolutely!

What opportunities are you missing in your organization to use stories of real experiences and real people, in place of the usual excel spreadsheet and slide presentation of the statistics that the story supports? Charts, statistics, and graphs are definitely important; but it's the backstory of those same elements that expands understanding, creates more emotional buy-in, identifies the vision and values of the group, and builds and expands the legacy of the contributing individuals as well as the organization.

Improving the Return on Influence results in:

- A more engaged team.
- Your "diamond in the rough" team members being encouraged to grow and try new things.
- Greater collaboration.
- Increased understanding.
- Leadership being exhibited by people who no one ever considered as a Leader

All of these points and more will provide an opportunity for the understanding to emerge.

We all have stories to share. We observe them every day, yet we forget to think about how a simple, everyday situation may be used to convey a business message that is important to the organization.

Take a look around. There are amazing examples waiting to be used and communicated. Put your spreadsheets aside occasionally. Look outside the walls that are covered with charts and graphs. Have fun looking for the obvious... it does not have to be "blinding."

"IMPRESS ME!"
A GLOBAL CONSTRUCTION
CONSULTANCY CASE STUDY

*"What you leave behind is not what is engraved in
stone monuments, but what is woven into the lives of others."*
– Pericles

When making a proposal to potential clients, expect that most of your audience would be aware, via word of mouth, of the expertise of the engineer and the company he represents; this speaks to the "Personality is the Brand" referred to earlier. That is merely the starting point; you should build on this foundation during the proposal presentation, and many times the best results come from an in person, face-to-face meeting.

Picture a hotel meeting room in the eastern part of the United States. Seven decision makers, representing the board of directors of the "buying" organization, make up the audience. Currently sitting with 6 feet of "social distancing" between them and wearing masks, they still give off a distinct feeling of combined power, and the expectation of waiting to be impressed.

Make no mistake: regardless of his belief in his own ability, the company behind him, the experience the project requires, the value this presentation will represent to this group, the organization behind them, and the results the project will deliver, this senior level engineer knew this was a specifically detailed presentation. It needed to influence this very corporate group from multiple countries and cultures in a very big way.

Initially one would think that the engineer presenting would seek to influence the potential buyers via the Buy-in level of our Influence Pyramid. After all, he is seeking belief in his vision for their construction project. And he definitely started at that level.

As the information became more technical and specific for the expected results required, the presentation meeting continued over several days. It even included a prototype of the completed structures to help the "audience" see things in 3D, and to ask more pertinent questions to better understand all the data the prototype represented.

Throughout all the questioning and clarifying necessarily required for the awarding of a contract worth millions of dollars, the feeling was still one of judgement and waiting to be "wowed!"

The engineer realized that to influence this potential sale, his message needed to be elevated to a more personal level, to show that it was the only option that would meet their requirements; perhaps it would even solve problems they didn't know they had.

Whether a proposal is for a hotel in China or a group of warehouses in the Middle East, it is all about how this specific project will add to or enhance the legacy of the buyer. With decades of experience in making proposals of this kind, this senior engineer intuitively understands that his proposal must influence at the Visionary Level of the Influence Pyramid.

The presentation must influence each member of this seven-member buyer group individually. Naturally, the engineer understands that this buyer group will reconvene privately each evening to share their thoughts with each other. Will they agree that this is "the answer" for their organization? Not being part of these private, after-hours sessions, our engineer knows he has done his best, but has he provided the level of influence necessary for them to say "yes?"

The nightly, private meetings provide the appropriate atmosphere for this seven-member panel to not only review the information presented, but to also influence each other. Will they influence each other negatively against the proposal; or positively to ensure that this is the best option for their organization?

As the meetings came to an end, the "impress us" wall of expectation had been breached. Everyone in the room seemed to be on the same page: looking to build something much bigger than themselves. The contractual issues were negotiated and addressed. The awarding of the contract, and the signing, became foregone conclusions, because our engineer elevated his message to appeal to the vision and the emotional need of leaving a legacy. He gave examples of similar projects from his previous experience, shared some of his identity and the connection that his experience provided to previous clients, who made their decisions based on their emotional need to contribute to the legacy of their respective organizations.

The way any organization does business, the methodologies they use, and their various ways of communication, reveal who they are at their core, and what they value. That is the power of influence both in good times and in challenging times.

As our world continues to change, business may or may not be done in exactly the same way we have always worked. Whether you view the "evolving normal" as a glass half empty or half full will determine how you can continue to influence your communities and constituencies at a higher level.

Powerful influence does not happen overnight, nor can it be mandated in the traditional sense. It takes commitment, an openness to exploring new options, and figuring out how you may use these opportunities. At the time of this writing (mid-pandemic 2020), we do not even know what our opportunities will look like. Without a doubt, they will be different and will require a dedication to working differently and more positively.

THE CHALLENGE CONTINUES: MAKING A REAL DIFFERENCE

"How wonderful is it that nobody need wait a single moment before starting to improve the world."
– Anne Frank

What portions of your journey are you sharing with your team?

What insights have you shared that provide the opportunity for others to "get it?"

Perhaps some of these story starters will help you think of specific stories you can share with your team/organization:

- When my son/daughter was _____ years old ...
- Learning to _____ taught me ...
- While traveling in _____ ...
- When purchasing my _____ ...

Assisting your team in "getting it" is the essence of leadership. Through engineering epiphanies by elevating your messages, you provide a greater platform for maximizing your ROI (Return on

Influence). The question becomes – which messages are coming through loud and clear? Have you elevated your messages often, and to a level that encourages others to be influenced differently?

Stories define who we are, what we believe, what we value, and how we behave. They allow us to influence others at a higher level, because the universal truths communicated are integrated into the lives we touch and live on through those lives. Creating lasting corporate stories solidifies corporate culture, creates corporate legends like *Little Timmy*, and identifies the heroes and "sheroes" within the organization. Using stories to illustrate, teach, inspire, engage, and connect are what influence and communication are all about.

THE AFTERMATH OF LITTLE TIMMY

"The universe is made up of stories, not of atoms."
– Muriel Rukeyser

A few weeks after *Little Timmy* had gone "to a better place," I was back at the plant. The plant manager and I had been discussing the coming week's activities, training, and coaching sessions. After concluding our discussion, he went back to his desk, leaving me to pack up my briefcase at the conference table at the rear of his large, L-shaped office.

As I was hoisting my briefcase onto my shoulder, one of the members of the senior management team came into the office, excited and agitated at the same time.

"Wow! What great information we got in the session with our major supplier. It was fantastic. He had all kinds of charts and graphs – the information was invaluable. We need to get it out to every employee on every shift." He paused and continued in a more conversational tone, "There's just one thing. We have to figure out a way to make it interesting, because it's too important not to communicate."

The plant manager asked a few questions, trying to decipher why his colleague was so concerned about making it interesting. If he was this excited, it had obviously interested him.

"It was just a very dry presentation," his team member explained. "It needed something to get folks to pay attention. In fact, I probably would not have paid as much attention as I did, but I knew you were expecting my report!"

The plant manager smiled, raised his eyebrows, and looked in my direction. Until then, this division manager was unaware that I was in the room. As soon as he saw me, he sat down, slapped his head, and said, "Of course, we need some stories!"

It was not that he didn't know about stories. He had been in that senior management training session a few weeks before, sharing a powerful story himself. The idea of "planning" to use stories, was not fully integrated into the daily operations (at least not yet). But with conscious effort, came thought; and with thought, came practice. The stories were there, waiting to be created or recalled, ready to be shared. It did not take long for the culture to reflect the change in communication and reap the benefits of elevating their messages for a greater return on their influence.

From a personal perspective, what opportunities do you have every day to share what you know, who you are, and the experiences you've had, to assist your colleagues, clients, customers and suppliers in learning and growing? What 'gators, like *Little Timmy*, lurk in your corporate pond that shouldn't be there? Are your people empowered to relocate them to a "better place?"

Change happens when we make our processes and procedures come alive by elevating our messages and using stories from our own experience to influence others understanding.

- What portions of your personal journey are you sharing with your team?

- What epiphanies are you engineering as a leader?
- What insights have you shared that provide the opportunity for others to "get it?"

Increasingly, leaders who invest time and effort in learning how to elevate their message will have opportunities to craft and tell stories that engage, teach, empower, and inspire. Their influence becomes stronger as they become more comfortable sharing their personal experiences.

THE AFTER STORY

"Through a story, life invites us to come inside as a participant."
– Stephen Denning

Perhaps this all sounds foreign, a waste of time. Perhaps you are thinking, "Hey, I'm not a leader, so what I say doesn't matter anyway."

Just as there is power in storytelling, there is power in brainstorming ideas with your colleagues, at whatever level you contribute toward the purpose and vision of your organization.

This is what happened after the supervisors in the room heard the story of *Little Timmy*. They heard other stories as well. They had a brief, collaborative, unscheduled brainstorming session to solve the problem. The young man who told the *Little Timmy* story did not come up with the solution. The story was the catalyst that prompted the conversation and the brainstorming to solve a problem they already knew about but had not been addressed at any level of management.

Whether you are a new hire or the CEO communicating through sharing relevant experiences (telling the story) and therefore elevating your message, those experiences can spur more creative problem solving, lateral thinking, and better buy-in throughout any organization or community (family, company, church, sports team, class, club, etc.). Isn't that what we do when we complain? We start a conversation with the words, "If I was running this organization…"

Remember the five levels of influence?

1. Compliance.
2. Participation.
3. Buy-in.
4. Leadership.
5. Visionary.

It is rare that we speak (whether orally, visually, or kinesthetically) to only one level at a time. Our organizations and teams are a mixture of all the levels. To maximize our ROI (Return on Influence), we need to continue to be conscious of elevating our messages. Sharing our own identities and journeys, as well as our corporate identities and journeys, promotes greater understanding and enhanced growth of our team members to higher levels of influence.

So, what is your story?

Will you live it and tell it well, allowing others to benefit from your authenticity and identity?

How will YOU begin?

Will your story have the influence and power of the well-chosen words from our handsome, young supervisor as he leaned forward and said the words that gave voice to many other elevated messages throughout the chemical plant?

"It was three o'clock in the morning…"

"AND IN SUMMARY . . ."

Years wrinkle the skin, but lack of enthusiasm wrinkles the soul!"
– Anonymous

Well here we are, at the end of our discussion about "elevating your messages to maximize your return on influence."

We have talked about:
- The Five Levels of Influence.
- The basic types of stories used most often in organizations.
- Engineering epiphanies.
- Results and the underlying importance of elevating our messages through sharing our personal experiences/stories.
- Sustainable methods for better communication and greater return on influence.
- Personality is the brand.
- Cost and results of NOT elevating your message.
- The continuing challenges of making a real difference.

Throughout our time together we shared multiple stories and experiences as examples of how to identify and use the Influence Pyramid.

We have covered a lot of ground in a short space for both you and the organizations and communities in which you participate.

So now what is next for you?

You have a very fundamental choice: you can either adapt what you've read to fit your model of the world, OR you can adapt your model of the world in light of this information.

I believe that what is true for organizations and communities is also true for individuals, especially those in leadership positions or who aspire to be in a leadership position:

- The market shall sit in judgment between the quick and the dead.
- The rich do not bury the poor, the creative bury the stagnant.
- The smart do not beat the dumb, the flexible beat the rigid.
- The strong don't crush the weak, the agile outperform the habitual.*

While you may think this is true, most people will not act on the information and ideas in this book. Harsh, perhaps; true, nonetheless.

Look around your organization. Many may be ambitious. How many of those are prepared to understand what is going on around them, to actually take an honest look at themselves, make a plan, share information about themselves, and then do the work to elevate their messages? For how many of them will YOU be a role model by elevating your messages?

The broadly accurate answer – not many!

Only you know the answer to the important question: Are you one of those who will elevate your message to have greater influence on those you work with and live with?

There's an old expression we've all heard, "When all is said and done, there's usually a lot more said than done." Many may intend; few will do.

This is just human nature. It is normal. You can be among the small percentage that makes a decision to take action, share your experiences, and actually realize a greater return on your influence. After all, the only things you know will not work, are the things you don't try!

Albert Schweitzer said, "Example is not the main thing in influencing others, it's the only thing!"

The thoughts, ideas, and strategies in this book are relatively easy to understand and implement. It is about the execution of good ideas.

If this was an enjoyable read, with some interesting information, and useful ideas, then we are both happy you have read the book.

Now the work begins. I am available to chat, to work with you and your organization, share ideas, and continue this conversation.

Let's start today! And I look forward to working with you as our journeys continue.

Thanks in advance,
Susan Luke Evans
susan@susanlukeevans.com
www.susanlukeevans.com
1-210-643-4367
Etobicoke, ON
Canada

Shared with and agreed between my late husband, Warren Evans and myself.

The sharing of these stories may be complete;
The journey of elevating your message to
Maximize Your Return on Influence,
like the message in this book continues...

**Do you want to share in a journey that
uncovers the stories you can share to
Maximize Your Return on Your Influence?**

Contact Susan Luke Evans

susan@susanlukeevans.com

Take advantage of individual or small group coaching

Invite Susan to Speak (Virtually or In Person)
to Your Organization

Invite Susan to Conduct Workshops for Your Team

Call: 1-210-643-4367

For additional copies of *Return on Influence*
order from Amazon

ABOUT THE AUTHOR

Susan Luke Evans is a leadership consultant and communications expert.

She is among 8% of Canadian speakers within the Canadian Association of Professional Speakers to hold their highest earned designation – the Certified Speaking Professional (CSP) and among less than 1% within the Global Speakers Federation to hold the Global Speaking Fellow designation.

Prior to starting her speaking business, Susan was CEO of a financial services support company where she executed a 5-year start-up plan in 3 years, distributed dividends a year ahead of schedule, and led a subsequent, highly successful merger.

Her practice centers on assisting leaders who want to elevate their messages to create flexible, engaged, and agile workplaces and in the process maximize their ROI (Return on Influence). She believes that everyone should LIVE a great Story to build their Legacy. She serves clients in over fifty countries on 6 continents.

She has held numerous leadership positions in national and international professional and philanthropic organizations.

Susan brings to her clients a unique combination of genuine expertise and powerful delivery. Her compelling information, practical ideas, positive approach, and irreverent sense of humor have garnered rave reviews around the world.

Giving a Voice to Creativity!

With every donation, a voice will be given to
the creativity that lies within the hearts of
our children living with diverse challenges.

By making this difference, children that may
not have been given the opportunity to have their
Heart Heard will have the freedom to create
beautiful works of art and musical creations.

Donate by visiting

HeartstobeHeard.com

We thank you.